MARMADUKE MULTIPLY'S

MERRY METHOD OF

MAKING MINOR

MATHEMATICIANS

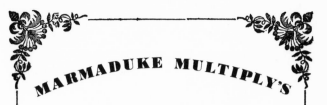

MARMADUKE MULTIPLY'S

MERRY METHOD OF

MAKING MINOR

MATHEMATICIANS

❧

Facsimile of the 1841 children's classic

With a new Preface and Bibliographic

Postscript by E. F. Bleiler

DOVER PUBLICATIONS, INC., NEW YORK

Published in Canada by General Publishing Company,
Ltd., 30 Lesmill Road, Don Mills, Toronto, Ontario.
Published in the United Kingdom by Constable and Company, Ltd., 10 Orange Street, London WC 2.

This Dover edition, first published in 1971, is a facsimile
(with one slight alteration) of the edition published by
Munroe and Francis in Boston in 1841. For the Dover
edition, E. F. Bleiler has written a new Preface and
Bibliographic Postscript.

International Standard Book Number: 0-486-20171-6
(clothbound)
International Standard Book Number: 0-486-22773-1
(paperbound)
Library of Congress Catalog Card Number: 70-170394

Manufactured in the United States of America
Dover Publications, Inc.
180 Varick Street
New York, N. Y. 10014

Preface to the Dover Edition

Marmaduke Multiply was originally published in England in 1816 and 1817 by John Harris. Copies came to America, and in the middle 1830's, perhaps 1836 or 1837, it was issued by Munroe and Francis of Boston, in a redesigned, Americanized edition. Joseph H. Francis may have done the revision, while Alonzo Hartwell was almost certainly responsible for the art work, preparing new woodcuts, based mostly on the illustrations for the British *Marmaduke Multiply*. The resulting book went through several printings without internal alteration. It was reprinted by James Miller of New York, who took over the Munroe and Francis properties, some time during the late 1860's or early 1870's. After this *Marmaduke Multiply* ceased to count for about one hundred years.

E . F . B L E I L E R

New York, 1971

MARMADUKE MULTIPLY.

BOSTON:

MUNROE AND FRANCIS.

1841.

Twice 1 are 2.

This book is something new.

Twice 2 are 4.

Pray hasten on before.

Twice **3** are **6**.

You're always playing tricks.

Twice 4 are 8.
Your bonnet is not straight.

Twice 5 are 10.

Look at my gallant men.

Twice 6 are 12.

I cannot find St. Elve.

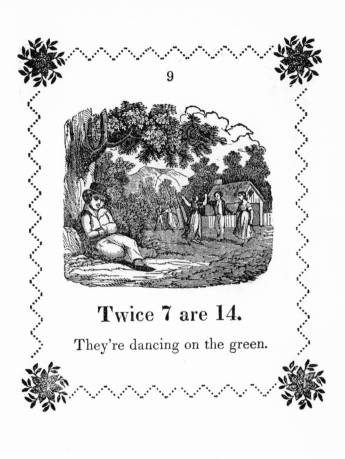

Twice 7 are 14.

They're dancing on the green.

Twice 8 are 16.

Yonder are lions to be seen.

Twice 9 are 18.

My Cow is very lean.

Twice **10** are **20**.

My purse is almost empty.

Twice 11 are 22.

Mister, can you mend my shoe?

Twice 12 are 24.

Mother haste, and ope the door.

3 times 1 are 3.

My darling, come to me.

3 times 2 are 6.

The man has brought some bricks.

3 times 3 are 9.

This boy's a friend of mine.

3 times 4 are 12.

I find no rhyme but delve.

3 times 5 are 15.

Lead the donkey on the green.

3 times 6 are 18.

How long they keep me waiting.

3 times 7 are 21.

Dear ma'am, pray see my dog and gun.

3 times 8 are 24.

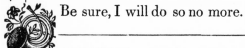

Be sure, I will do so no more.

3 times 9 are 27.

I hear the clock, it strikes eleven

3 times 10 are 30.

My face is very dirty.

3 times 11 are 33.

Jack and Bill have gone to sea.

3 times 12 are 36.

We'll hide our Cakes behind the ricks.

4 times 4 are 16.

The air to-day is very keen.

4 times 5 are 20.

Jack says his purse is empty.

4 times 6 are 24.

I think I've seen your face before.

4 times 7 are 28.

Come with me and see me skate.

4 times 8 are 32.

I once could dance as well as you.

4 times 9 are 36.

Your medicine I soon will mix.

4 times 10 are 40.

Those boys are very naughty.

4 times 11 are 44.

I bought this book at Francis'.
Store.

4 times **12** are **48.**

I wish that I could get some bait.

5 times 5 are 25.

I thank my stars I'm yet alive.

5 times 6 are 30.

She's tall as any fir-tree.

5 times 7 are 35.

The Chickens are safe beneath the hive.

5 times 8 are 40.

That man is very haughty.

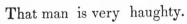

5 times 9 are 45.

We're going with Tom to take a drive.

5 times 10 are 50.

My Rose is very thrifty.

5 times 11 are 55.

I see the chaise, they'll soon arrive.

5 times 12 are 60.

The house is like a pig-sty.

6 times 6 are 36.

This pretty bird is cousin Dick's.

6 times 7 are 42.

This is the Road that leads to Looe.

6 times 8 are 48.

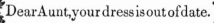

Dear Aunt, your dress is out of date.

6 times 9 are 54.

My little boat has come ashore.

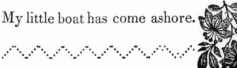

6 times 10 are 60.

This pretty shawl will fix me.

6 times 11 are 66.

O see that Horse, how high he kicks.

6 times 12 are 72.

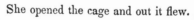

She opened the cage and out it flew.

7 times 7 are 49.

I dry my clothes upon a line.

7 times 8 are 56.

That fellow merits twenty kicks.

7 times 9 are 63.

Come, pray sir, give that hat to me.

7 times 10 are 70.

We're sailing very pleasantly.

7 times 11 are 77.

I always make my bread with leaven

7 times 12 are 84.

O happy little tawny Moor.

8 times 8 are 64.

A Baron bold in days of yore.

8 times 9 are 72.

Come here, I'll show you where they grew.

8 times 10 are 80.

I think he's pretty weighty.

8 times 11 are 88.

If you fall down, you'll break your pate.

8 times 12 are 96.

My wandering thoughts I cannot fix.

9 times 9 are 81.

See how fast those horses run.

9 times 10 are 90.

Now you shall taste my fine Tea.

9 times 11 are 99.

 This bunch of grapes grew on my vine.

9 times 12 are 108.

See what I've drawn upon my slate.

10 times 10 are 100.

How he got there, they wondered.

Ten times 11 are 110.

Charles has made me a very good pen.

10 times 12 are 120.

I laugh, and sing, and live in plenty.

Eleven times 11 are 121.

Come here, little boy, and buy a nice bun.

Eleven times **12** are **132**.

Buy my clothes, old and new.

12 times 12 are 144.

So I bid you good bye, and shut the door.

In Quest of Marmaduke Multiply

A Bibliographic Postscript

In Quest of Marmaduke Multiply

A Bibliographic Postscript

i

In the fall of 1970 one of the most charming early American children's books turned up at auction in New York. This was a copy of the extremely rare Munroe and Francis edition of *Marmaduke Multiply*, published in Boston in 1841. Well-planned, with a consistent series of excellent wood engravings, it was one of the finest examples of early inexpensive book making.

Marmaduke Multiply has long been well-known to specialists in children's literature, but only as a rare book in a few large collections. It has never been studied, and it has not been reprinted within the past hundred years. Even such great collections as the Library of Congress, the Osborne Collection of

Toronto, and the Sinclair Hamilton Collection at Princeton do not own copies of the American edition. It has been known mostly through a partial reproduction in Tuer's *Stories from Old-Fashioned Children's Books,* where the British text is followed, and an excerpt in Arnold Arnold's *Pictures and Stories from Forgotten Children's Books,* where a later American edition is used. Even these brief evidences, however, have revealed it as a book worthy to stand beside *Peter Piper* as a fanciful educational aid. It demonstrates that the twentieth century has no monopoly on imagination in education.

No records of the American *Marmaduke Multiply* survive, and it has been necessary to work with the book itself, its illustrations, and its text, to determine its origin and publication history. Since materials are scattered and are largely held together by inference, this history turned out to be a gradual investigation, sometimes exasperating and frustrating, sometimes perplexing and misleading, but always filled with a small thrill of discovery. It became a minor detective story of the nursery.

ii

Twice 1 are 2,
This book is something new.

This is not really true. A brief check of bibliographic sources showed that *Marmaduke Multiply*
first appeared in England, in parts published in
1816 and 1817. It was issued by John Harris of St.
Paul's Churchyard, London, the successor to the
famous John Newbery who had been the foremost
children's publisher in the eighteenth century. Just
who first prepared *Marmaduke Multiply* is not
known; possibly it was Harris himself. As far as
could be determined, no prototypes or predecessors
existed, although around the time of the first British
edition one-two-buckle-my-shoe rhymes and toy
books were especially prevalent, and an occasional
rhyme foreshadowed a more elaborate use of numbers for children. Gumuchian lists a book, *Nursery
Calculations, Or, A Peep into Numbers* (circa

1815?), which contains such rhymes as:

> Three dozen counts for thirty-six
>   They're naughty boys who fight with sticks

> One hundred shillings make five pound,
>   In gamester's pockets, seldom found

and, of course, John Harris himself had offered *Peter Piper's Practical Principles* to the market not too long before.

The American counterpart to Newbery and Harris was the firm of Munroe and Francis in Boston, who issued the present edition of *Marmaduke Multiply*. They were the children's publishers par excellence for the second quarter of the nineteenth century, and many of their books created repercussions that continue to this day. They produced many collections of nursery material, including the famous 1833 *Mother Goose's Melodies* which established Mother Goose as the children's poet for all American future history, and they also published *Parley's Magazine*, which was the foremost children's magazine of the late 1830's. Associated with the publishing house— exact linkages not clear—was the bookshop of J. H.

Munroe and Francis Book Store

Francis on Washington Street, Boston. A related establishment existed in New York on Broadway, the book store of C. S. Francis, who was a cousin.

> 4 times 11 are 44.
> I bought this book at Francis's store.

Marmaduke Multiply is a small exemplar of the concern that early America had with education, particularly mathematics. Book after book was offered to the American public, some of British origin, some of American. Indeed, a bibliography of such books printed before 1850, by the historian of science Karpinski, runs to more than 450 pages. Most of these books were elementary, usually mercantile in approach.

With this great an interest in elementary mathematics, it is not surprising that there were occasional novel approaches to teaching. While we tend to think of the education of this period as being a sterile continuation of the past, this is only a partial picture. There were Pestalozzian groups in the East and the Middle West, and Bronson Alcott and others taught experimentally in the Boston area. Before *Marmaduke Multiply* appeared in America there were a couple of books that taught the multiplication table in verse, although they were of no historical importance. There were geometric recreations, such as the earliest known tangram book, and many other ways to teach or learn arithmetic joyfully, painlessly, accurately, and economically. Almost every new arithmetic made some such claim.

In the immediate forefront of this mathematical ferment was Samuel G. Goodrich, better known as Peter Parley, whose *Method of Teaching Arithmetic to Children* was published in Boston in 1833 and went through many editions. Parley, who is regarded with loathing by lovers of Mother Goose, sounds very modern:

I have here attempted to write a book of arithmetic, that shall prove as amusing to children, as a book of stories. Arithmetic is generally repulsive, not, as I believe, from any native antipathy, but from a disgust engendered by the disagreeable form in which it is usually presented to children . . . [who] may be likened to flowering plants, that only acquire perfection in a genial soil.

Parley, however, did not anticipate the other trend in modern elementary mathematics, the foundational, algebraic New Mathematics, but remained on a concrete level:

How many claws, tails, and noses have 4 lions?

If 6 Indians can live upon a buffalo for a month, how many Indians can live for a month upon three buffaloes?

A skunk went into a barn where he found 3 nests; one had 7 eggs, another 8, and another 3; from each nest the skunk ate 2 eggs; now tell me how many eggs were in the three nests? How many eggs did the skunk eat? How many eggs were left after he had finished his supper?

It was against this background of intense interest in the simpler forms of mathematics that *Marmaduke Multiply* was revived and remodeled in Boston, some time in the middle 1830's. Munroe and Francis, who had clear ideas about the value of nursery rhymes, in contradiction to Parley, and were progressive, may have felt that they were accomplishing a worthwhile end in introducing *Marmaduke* to America.

iii

The American *Marmaduke Multiply* is a unit-book, obviously planned and executed according to a consistent pattern. In this respect it is superior to most early nineteenth-century children's paperbacks, which often appear to have been thrown together haphazardly. Who was responsible for its design? Records reveal nothing. Our only clue is an initial H, slanted and simple, which is concealed in the shadows of three illustrations: those on pages 13, 34, and 42. The other cuts are not identified, but most of them seem obviously from the same hand.

This same H had appeared in the Munroe and Francis *Mother Goose's Melodies,** where the artist had similarly initialed the shadows of a smithy and a hobbyhorse. At that time the search for H had narrowed itself down to two major claimants, John H. Hall and Alonzo Hartwell. Hall, a New Yorker who had learned wood engraving from Alexander Anderson, and often signed his work JHH, later

---

*Facsimile published by Dover Publications, Inc., 1970.

became an associate of Abel Bowen's in Boston. Alonzo Hartwell (1805–1873) had been a pupil of Bowen's. Both men worked in the Boston area in the 1830's, and had associations with Munroe and Francis.

Sinclair Hamilton's magnificent *Early American Book Illustrators and Wood Engravers*, although it does not contain *Marmaduke Multiply*, offered several leads for deciding the identity of H on stylistic grounds. It catalogues many books and periodicals illustrated by Hall and Hartwell, although most of these books, on inspection, did not help much: their illustrations were mostly architectural or portrait or miscellaneous. Eventually, however, enough signed material for both Hall and Hartwell turned up to identify the artist of *Marmaduke Multiply* with a fair degree of certainty.

John H. Hall composed a fine series of comparable illustrations for Lydia M. Child's *Girl's Own Book* (Boston, 1833). Hall showed himself to be a very competent engraver, skilled at infusing motion, grace, and lightness into his cuts. Under the lens, indeed, Hall's moving figures and flowing drapes even had a Botticellian suggestion at times.

His textures, perspective and composition, however, were less skilled than those of H. The more work by Hall was examined, the more obvious it became that Hall could not be H.

Parley's Magazine, which was published by the Francises of Boston in the late 1830's and early 1840's, turned out to be decisive for Alonzo Hartwell. An excellent children's magazine, it contained illustrations signed by H and similar illustrations signed in full by Hartwell. Both groups of illustrations shared certain features: a technique more adapted to the woodblock than Hall's was at times; a fine use of texture, almost as good as Bewick's own work; good composition; and occasionally an astonishing creation of depth perspective. Hartwell and H also shared two faults. Neither could express motion, except in a strained manner, and their work is usually static. And both had the same difficulties with the human figure. Whereas Hall could suggest grace and Alexander Anderson (whose work was also present) could draw a slim figure that revealed bone and muscle beneath the clothing, Hartwell and H drew a dumpy person with balloon clothing and a peculiar posture suggestive of spinal problems.

Stylistically, Hartwell and H were almost identical, and it is safe to assume that Alonzo Hartwell was at least the major artist in this book.

In *Marmaduke Multiply* an amusing touch is to be found in the house and furnishings assigned to the living numbers. As can be seen from several cuts, it was a pillared, Greek Revival house with interior white paneled doors, a Bulfinch staircase with a radish post, a simple paneled fireplace mantle with a Franklin grate, and it was furnished mostly in Empire style, often reminiscent of Duncan Phyfe. The curved legs of the chairs, the rayed front to the secretary are consistent, as is the garden house with the diamond windows and the Tom Sawyer fence. Much the same house, surrounded with a border like those in *Marmaduke Multiply*, occurs in *Parley's Magazine*, signed in full by Hartwell. It is an interesting speculation that this was Hartwell's own house that served as a model, and that possibly it still stands in Littleton, Massachusetts, where Hartwell lived.

iv

Parley's Magazine, besides offering evidence that
H was Alonzo Hartwell, created a temporary problem. From 1838 to 1841 *Parley's Magazine* printed
the individual illustrations from *Marmaduke Multiply,* without the borders, with a different text.
The January, 1838, issue, for example, shows the
little girl holding a book, as on page 34 here, but
with the text, "I wish you all a happy New Year,/
Plenty of books and very good cheer." This was
followed by the skating scene of page 30, with the
new verse, "Every season brings its joy.—/I'm for
skating now, my boy." The illustration from page
19 served "Old Dobbin," a poem by Miss Eliza
Cook, and page 43 illustrated, not too well, "Patty
Proud." Usually the cuts fit the letterpress well
enough, although there are some exceptions, such
as the cut showing the road to Looe (page 45),
which was used to illustrate an article about Bruce
the traveler.

The question immediately arose: were the cuts in
Marmaduke Multiply originally a miscellaneous

series, which Munroe and Francis used in *Parley's Magazine* and for the number verses? Or were the blocks from *Marmaduke Multiply* cannibalized for the magazine? In terms of inner logic the balance was about even: some illustrations fitted *Marmaduke Multiply* better; others fitted the text in *Parley's Magazine* better.

This problem reflected a curious episode in book publishing, a situation that was almost unique to the technology of the early nineteenth century. At the end of the eighteenth century, Thomas Bewick of England had developed a method for engraving a very detailed image on the endgrain of hard, fine wood, thereby creating a printing block that could stand almost indefinite impressions. It could be combined with type more easily than the earlier copperplate engravings, and it was cheaper and easier to prepare. By the nature of the wood used —boxwood—small illustrations usually squarish in shape became the rule. After the turn of the nineteenth century American book illustration followed Bewick's technique closely, and also imitated his subject matter and artistic mannerisms.

It now became practical for a book publisher to

build up a reference store of wood blocks which he could easily move from one book to another. If a new book needed illustrations, blocks could be taken from the archives and tied up with the type. This, of course, was an economy measure, and interlocked with it was a tendency to keep illustrations generalized enough to fit many situations, whence the haphazard illustration of many early nineteenth-century books. Another result is that individual blocks can sometimes be traced from book to book within a publisher's line. When such reanimations are combined with the pervasiveness of the Bewick style and the anonymity of most work, the twentieth-century reader is often at a loss to date or pinpoint an illustration. Perhaps this is a trivial point, not likely to disturb anyone but a professional bibliographer, but it does hamper our understanding of artists and book histories.

Munroe and Francis specialized in this sort of embellishment. In a notice printed in *Parley's Magazine,* they boast of "facilities in new or already accumulated engravings, which no other publishers possess, and this store of pictures is increasing every day." These resources enabled them to print children's books with hundreds of illustrations, like their *Little Child's Book*, a collection of fairy tales with more than 400 pictures. For the researcher, however, this is a nuisance, for one can find *Mother Goose* cuts serving equally well in the 1835 printing of Ann Taylor's *Select Rhymes for the Nursery* and illustrating odd poems in *Parley's Magazine*, and one can find *Marmaduke Multiply* cuts in the 1844 *Original Poems for Infant Minds*. Thus, although illustration is sometimes our only clue to circumstances of publication, it can be a very misleading clue.

The origin of the illustrations in *Marmaduke Multiply* was soon settled, however, by the arrival of xeroxes of the British edition: *Marmaduke Multiply's Merry Method of Making Minor Mathematicians*. A small book, roughly the same size as the American edition, it was printed completely from copper plates, even to the lettering. These same plates, indeed, were used on up to the 1840's, and late copies can be distinguished from early by watermarks on the paper.

The illustrations in the British edition, which were nicely colored by hand, were in the broadside and catchpenny tradition of the late eighteenth and early nineteenth centuries, stylistically different from the wood engravings of Hartwell. Yet the subject matter is often the same in both books, and it is obvious that Hartwell had a copy of the British edition before him when he prepared his blocks. Most of his cuts are clearly suggested by their British counterparts, although Hartwell changed them radically, adding backgrounds, reinterpreting personalities, and creating a consistent mood that the British edition did not have. The over-all impression that one receives is that while Harris's is a city book, Hartwell's is a country or small-town book.

A curious element in Hartwell's reinterpretation is that he often reversed left and right from the British edition. This immediately raises the question whether another state of *Marmaduke Multiply* existed between the original Harris and Hartwell. In older engravings a stolen illustration often came out in reverse: one glued a print face down upon a copper plate, scraped until the image could be seen from the rear, then cut into the metal. Hartwell may have worked from such a reverse edition, although no trace of any such edition has turned up. Without such evidence, we can only say that Hartwell arbitrarily reversed many plates.

The likenesses between the Harris and the American editions make it certain that Hartwell drew his illustrations specially for the book, and that Francis borrowed them for his periodical. This was probably done via stereo plates, since the lockup on all copies of the book is precisely the same.*

A few illustrations in *Marmaduke Multiply*, however, were not derived from the British prototype. The peddler on page 70, for example, is obviously taken from a collection of street cries, and other illustrations may have been suggested by primers. The borders were also new, being foundry cuts generally available to the trade. Munroe and Francis used certain of these same borders in their edition of the *New Hieroglyphick Bible*, in which Hartwell also had a hand.

---

*Stereotypy seems to have been more common in early American printing than is generally known. An amusing instance of this emerged during the search for publication notices for *Marmaduke Multiply*. The *Boston Pearl* for 1837 published a list of deadbeat subscribers, threatening to repeat the list "in stereotype" until the bills were paid.

V

Just as Alonzo Hartwell reworked the illustrations
for the American edition, someone in the editorial
department of Munroe and Francis reworked the
British verses for a new social and national market.
While the editor retained the now cryptic verse
about Looe (well-known in the early nineteenth
century as a Cornish market town), he rejected
many Anglicisms:

> Twice 11 *are* 22
> We'll drink to the Hero of Waterloo.

became

> Twice 11 are 22.
> Mister, can you mend my shoe?

Similarly, an anti-British note enters in the illustration to "5 times 8 are forty/ That man is very
haughty." It is obviously a picture of Wellington.

> 3 times 9 *are* 27
> My Babes and I are going to Devon.

became

> 3 times 9 are 27.
> I hear the clock, it strikes eleven,

where Hartwell's clock is set at 11 o'clock.

Certain elements of high life were apparently considered improper for the children of Boston circa 1835:

> 6 times 11 *are* 66
> We're four by Honours, and three by tricks

with an illustration showing a mixed foursome playing cards became

> 6 times 11 are 66.
> O, see that Horse, how high he kicks.

Wine-bibbing yielded to domestic virtue:

> 7 times 7 *are* 49
> You'll say, I think, this is good wine.

became

> 7 times 7 are 49.
> I dry my clothes upon a line.

The rural note enters:

9 times 11 *are* 99
See Sophy how my ear-rings shine.

is altered to

9 times 11 are 99.
This bunch of grapes grew on my vine.

All this leads up to

4 times 11 *are* 44
Pray make this noise my dears no more,

as transmogrified into

4 times 11 are 44.
I bought this book at Francis' store.

We do not know who made these changes, although the indications would seem to favor Joseph H. Francis of Boston as the sponsor for the children's books. It is always possible, however, that he had assistance. At the time that *Marmaduke Multiply* was prepared, Bronson Alcott worked for the company, editing *Parley's Magazine*. He may just possibly have had a hand in *Marmaduke Multiply*, which would fit his theories of education.

vi

It would have been satisfying to determine the exact date that *Marmaduke Multiply* first appeared in America, but this has not been possible. No notices were to be found in the Boston and New York newspapers that were available, nor were the books themselves decisive. Only a half-dozen copies of the Munroe and Francis editions of *Marmaduke Multiply* are to be traced in public libraries, and none is earlier than the Dover 1841 copy. A bookseller's catalogue of a few years back listed an 1839 printing, which is the earliest date now known, although there is no reason to claim this for the first edition.

Negative evidence, however, suggests that *Marmaduke Multiply* may have appeared around 1837. The *American Monthly Review*, which habitually noticed Munroe and Francis books, does not mention *Marmaduke Multiply*. It suspended publication in 1834, merging with the *New England Magazine*. The mass appearance of the engravings in *Parley's Magazine* in 1838 also suggests that *Marmaduke Multiply* had already been published. It would seem more reasonable to reprint illustrations from a book that had already been published than to jeopardize sale of an unpublished book that depended heavily on its picture material. This suggests 1836 or 1837, although such a date is only supposition.

A bibliographic ghost appeared and had to be laid during this checking of editions. The rare-book room of the New York Public Library owns a defective copy of *Marmaduke Multiply*, which its cardfile dates as 183–. This dating is not based on a printed date within the book, but on an almost effaced pencil notation on the wrapper: Mary Emery (?), 18–5. The third numeral is almost worn away, but it looks like a 3. The publisher is Charles S. Francis and Co., of New York, the cousin organization to Munroe and Francis of Boston.

The first thrill that emerged on seeing what might have been the only surviving copy of a first edition was qualified by a recognition that something was wrong. The paper was not the good paper of the earlier Munroe and Francis books, but a cheap stock, such as they used in later years. The cartouche on the cover looked very Victorian, rather than of the 1830's. And C. S. Francis did not become a company until 1842. Could it still be assumed that *Marmaduke Multiply* was in print in 1835?

At this point luck entered the investigation. The librarian kindly volunteered the information that the library owned another, uncatalogued copy of *Marmaduke Multiply*, stored in the same book box as the "1835" edition. This copy turned out to be a James Miller printing, undated, but from the back ads obviously from the late 1860's or 1870.

A type examination showed a sequence of editions among the Dover copy, the "1835" copy, and the Miller edition. All three books (a glance and a few measurements showed) came from the same lockup. The same breaks occurred in the rules, the same precise dimensions. Under the glass, however, the "1835" edition was obviously between the Dover copy and the Miller edition in type degeneration. The Miller copy showed type defects that were present in "1835" but not in the Dover copy: a missing tail from the "y" on page 18, a weak dotted "i" on page 31. There were many such points, although the paper was poor enough that one could not be sure at times what was bad presswork and what was breakdown of type.

The result, however, was the inescapable conclusion that the New York Public Library copy was a very late printing, and that the questionable date should be read "1855," since it obviously could not be "1845." An advertisement in another book published by C. S. Francis later revealed that *Marmaduke Multiply* was still in print with Francis of New York in 1856. It was available in a colored edition (no copy presently known) for 38 cents and a plain edition for 15 cents. All this, unfortunately, while removing a ghost book from the records, was of no real help in tracing the first printing of *Marmaduke Multiply*.

It was probably the success of the Munroe and Francis *Marmaduke Multiply*, which must have gone through at least six printings (and perhaps more) before the Miller edition, that created a pair of unsuccessful imitations in the 1840's. One was the *Lu Lu Multiplier*, issued by the New York publisher Samuel Raynor. One of a series rather vaguely associated with a girl named Lu Lu, it is a close imitation of *Marmaduke Multiply*, interesting in itself, but inferior in both verse and illustration. It seems to have been printed only once.

A logical extension of the rhymed tables was provided in *The Multiplication Table in Rhyme, for Young Arithmeticians*, published by Kiggins and Kellogg of New York. A toy book, only 3 inches by 4½ inches, it connected the individual rhymes into little stories and moral treatises:

LITTLE JANE.

Four times one are four,
Little Jane was very poor;
Four times two are eight,
And on others had to wait;
Four times three are twelve,
In the garden she would delve. . . .

THE FATHER'S ADVICE.

Ten times two are twenty,
Be not grasping when you've plenty;
Ten times three are thirty,
For niggard tricks are mean and dirty;
Ten times four are forty,
Be not presuming, vain, or haughty. . . .

Ten times eleven are a hundred ten,
Good boys will make the best of men;
   Ten times twelve are a hundred twenty,
And thus continue permanently.

vii

The results of this brief literary detective work are as follows: *Marmaduke Multiply* was originally published in England in 1816 and 1817 by John Harris. Copies came to America, and in the middle 1830's, perhaps 1837, it was issued by Munroe and Francis of Boston in a redesigned, Americanized edition. Joseph H. Francis may have done the revision, while Alonzo Hartwell was almost certainly responsible for the art work. Hartwell prepared new woodcuts, based mostly on the British illustrations for *Marmaduke Multiply*. The resulting book went through several printings without internal alteration. It was last reprinted by James Miller of New York, who took over the Munroe and Francis properties, some time during the late 1860's or early 1870's. After this *Marmaduke Multiply* ceased to count for about one hundred years.

E. F. BLEILER

New York, 1971

Acknowledgments

Gratitude must be expressed to Arnold Arnold for access to his copy of the Miller edition; Miss Judith St. John, Librarian of the Osborne Collection, Children's House, Toronto Public Library, Canada, for information on the Osborne copy of the British *Marmaduke*; the New York State Library, Albany, for photographic prints; the New York Public Library, New York City, for access to rare juveniles; Princeton University Library, Princeton, New Jersey, for access to the Sinclair Hamilton Collection, and for the unique print of Francis's bookstore.